The Natural History Museum
Weird & Wonderful Guides

Zooming
and
Creeping

Barbara Taylor

W9-CSK-733

PETER BEDRICK BOOKS

Acknowledgments

The publishers would like to thank:

Marwell Zoological Park, National Birds of Prey Centre, Weymouth Sealife Park,
Chelsea Physic Garden, Kings Reptile World, Virginia Cheeseman, Mark O'Shea and the
following staff at The Natural History Museum, London: Barry Bolton, Steve Brooks, Paul Clark,
Barry Clarke, Paul Cornelius, Oliver Crimmen, Peter Forey, Frank Greenaway, Richard Harbord, Daphne Hills,
Paul Hillyard, Paula Jenkins, Carol Levick, Judith Marshall, Colin McCarthy, Angela Milner, Fred Naggs,
Cally Oldershaw, Gordon Paterson, Robert Press, Robert Prys-Jones, Gaden Robinson, Andrew Smith,
Chris Stanley, Frank Steinheimer, John Taylor, Kathie Way, the staff of the EM Unit,
Photo Unit, Picture Library and Publishing Division.

Photography copyright © The Natural History Museum, except the following:
p. 12 b copyright © BBC Natural History Unit (Michael and Patricia Fogden)
p. 15 tr copyright © BBC Natural History Unit (Martha Holmes)
p. 18 copyright © BBC Natural History Unit (Jeff Foot)
p. 20 main copyright © FLPA (Dr. S.B. Idso)
p. 21 copyright © FLPA (D. Hoadley)
p. 20 bl copyright © Katz Pictures (Tomasz Tomaszewski/Visum)
p. 6 b copyright © Oxford Scientific Films
p. 7 tr copyright © Tim Knight
p. 8 b copyright © Natural History Photographic Agency (Stephen Dalton)
p. 19 copyright © Science Photo Library (Martin Bond)
New photography by Frank Greenaway

The creatures in this book are not reproduced life size, or to scale.

This Americanized Edition of *Zooming and Creeping* originally published in English
in 2001 is published in arrangement with Oxford University Press.

Published in the United States in 2001 by Peter Bedrick Books
A division of NTC/Contemporary Publishing Group, Inc.
4255 West Touhy Avenue, Lincolnwood (Chicago), Illinois 60712-1975 U.S.A.
Text copyright © Barbara Taylor 2000

All rights reserved. No part of this book may be reproduced, stored in a retrieval system,
or transmitted in any form or by any means, electronic, mechanical, photocopying, recording,
or otherwise, without the prior written permission of the copyright holders.

Printed in China

International Standard Book Number: 0-87226-657-5

10 9 8 7 6 5 4 3 2 1
Library of Congress Cataloging-in-Publication Data
Taylor, Barbara, 1954-
Zooming and creeping / Barbara Taylor.
p. cm. — (The Natural History Museum weird and wonderful guides)
ISBN 0-87226-657-5
1. Animals—Miscellanea—Juvenile literature. 2. Animal locomotion—Juvenile literature.
(1. Animal locomotion)
I. Title. II. Series.
QL49 .T2163 2001
573.7'9—dc21   00-56490

Contents

Animal Olympics

Can you imagine being able to sprint faster than a car, swim faster than a boat, and fly faster than a plane? Some animals can do all these things, and would easily win races if they entered the human Olympics.

Narrow, pointed wings for super speed.

A peregrine falcon is the fastest animal in the whole world. When it dives down to catch a bird it goes as fast as 124 miles per hour.

The cheetah is the fastest land animal over short distances, but it has to stop after about a minute because it gets so hot. After a fast chase, a cheetah may take 20 minutes to cool down.

Backbone bends up and down as the

Claws stick out to grip the ground like spiked running shoes.

Did You Know ?

An ostrich can sprint 328 feet in just 5 seconds - phew!

The black mamba snake slithers along at 10 feet per second.

A squid can dart through the water at nearly 68 miles per hour.

Hawk moths zoom about on their pointed wings like tiny jet aircraft. They can reach speeds of up to 24 miles per hour.

The sailfish is the fastest fish in the sea. It has a pointed nose and a streamlined shape, so it can swim at over 62 miles per hour.

cheetah runs, so it can take extra long strides.

All four legs are off the ground for a split second.

Long thin legs with powerful muscles.

Runners and jumpers

An animal moving on land pushes backwards against the ground to move forwards. Fast-moving animals often have long legs to take big strides. They also have powerful muscles that give them an extra push for speeding along. Jumping is a quick and efficient way of moving. Energy stored in the legs can be quickly released, to catapult the animal into the air.

Ostriches are the fastest two-legged runners in the animal world. They can reach speeds of nearly 45 miles per hour. They run mainly on one big toe on each foot. Their long legs have big muscles at the top.

Did You Know?

A bottlenose dolphin can leap up to 20 feet into the air.

The European hare can run at up to 30 miles per hour, for up to 15 minutes. This helps it to survive in areas where there are few places to hide.

This basilisk lizard escapes predators by running on water! It moves at 6 miles per hour so that its fast feet do not have time to sink under the water.

Powerful back legs end in long, fringed toes like flippers.

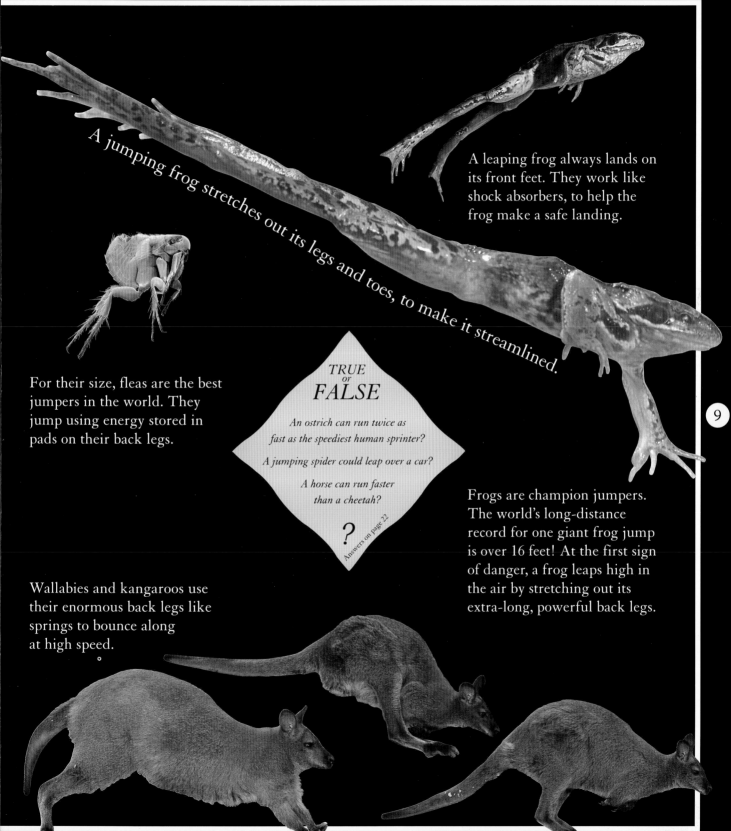

A jumping frog stretches out its legs and toes, to make it streamlined.

A leaping frog always lands on its front feet. They work like shock absorbers, to help the frog make a safe landing.

For their size, fleas are the best jumpers in the world. They jump using energy stored in pads on their back legs.

TRUE
or
FALSE

An ostrich can run twice as fast as the speediest human sprinter?

A jumping spider could leap over a car?

A horse can run faster than a cheetah?

?

Answers on page 22

Frogs are champion jumpers. The world's long-distance record for one giant frog jump is over 16 feet! At the first sign of danger, a frog leaps high in the air by stretching out its extra-long, powerful back legs.

Wallabies and kangaroos use their enormous back legs like springs to bounce along at high speed.

Creeping and crawling

Animals that glide or scuttle along close to the ground may have five legs, hundreds of legs - or no legs at all. They travel using the power of their muscles, or the pressure of fluids in their feet or bodies. They may not be the speediest creatures, but they have other ways of escaping their enemies.

Caterpillars like this one are called loopers. Holding on with their back legs, they move their front end as far forward as possible. Then they arch up into a loop, bringing the back end forward to meet the front.

Looper caterpillars have no legs at all in the middle part of their body.

Starfish move on hundreds of tiny tube feet. Each foot is like a small balloon, filled with seawater, that ends in a sticky sucker. The feet get longer when more water is forced into them, and shorter when they have less water inside.

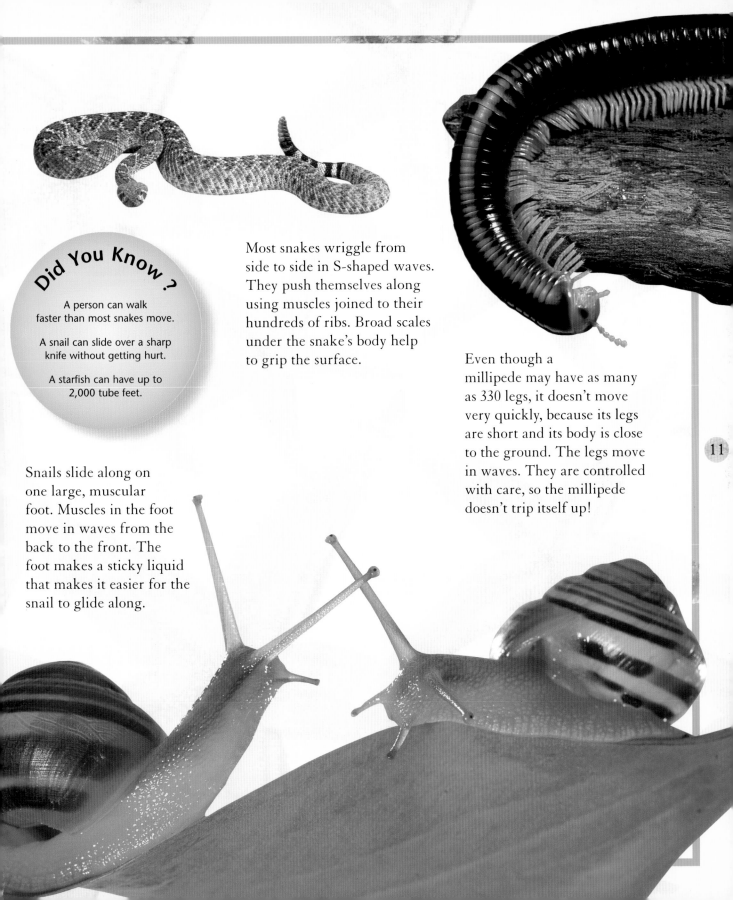

Did You Know ?

A person can walk faster than most snakes move.

A snail can slide over a sharp knife without getting hurt.

A starfish can have up to 2,000 tube feet.

Most snakes wriggle from side to side in S-shaped waves. They push themselves along using muscles joined to their hundreds of ribs. Broad scales under the snake's body help to grip the surface.

Even though a millipede may have as many as 330 legs, it doesn't move very quickly, because its legs are short and its body is close to the ground. The legs move in waves. They are controlled with care, so the millipede doesn't trip itself up!

Snails slide along on one large, muscular foot. Muscles in the foot move in waves from the back to the front. The foot makes a sticky liquid that makes it easier for the snail to glide along.

Fliers and gliders

Imagine you are a tiny hummingbird, whizzing along so fast that your wings are just a blur. Or that your arms have turned into a bat's skinny wings, to flap gracefully through the night air. Our aeroplanes, helicopters and gliders are just clumsy machines compared with the speed and agility of animal fliers and gliders.

A hummingbird's wings make a humming sound.

Dragonflies are among the world's fastest flying insects. They zoom to and fro at up to 20 miles per hour, scooping up gnats and other flying insects with their long, trailing legs.

Hummingbirds can hover, move from side to side, go straight up, straight down, and even fly backwards, like tiny helicopters.

A bat's wing is a hand made up of stretched-out fingers joined by leathery skin.

Fast-flying bats, such as this noctule bat, have long, thin wings. Bats fly rather like a swimmer doing the butterfly stroke. They can reach speeds of almost 30 miles per hour in the open.

Did You Know?

A hummingbird beats its wings up to 75 times a second.

Flying fish can glide for about 1,600 feet above the surface of the sea.

Swifts can sleep while they are flying.

This gecko doesn't need a parachute! The flaps of skin along the sides of its body work like a parachute when spread out, so the gecko can glide from tree to tree without falling to the ground.

Speedy swimmers

Would you like to be able to swim ten times faster than an Olympic champion? A blue marlin fish can swim this fast. The speediest swimmers in the animal world have strong muscles and a smooth, pointed body shape, with flippers and fins instead of fingers and toes. Some use special swimming skills such as jet propulsion.

Mackerel have a highly streamlined body shape and look rather like striped torpedoes. They bend their large tail fin from side to side, to shoot along at top speeds of about 13 miles per hour.

Wing-like front fins help the shark to stay afloat.

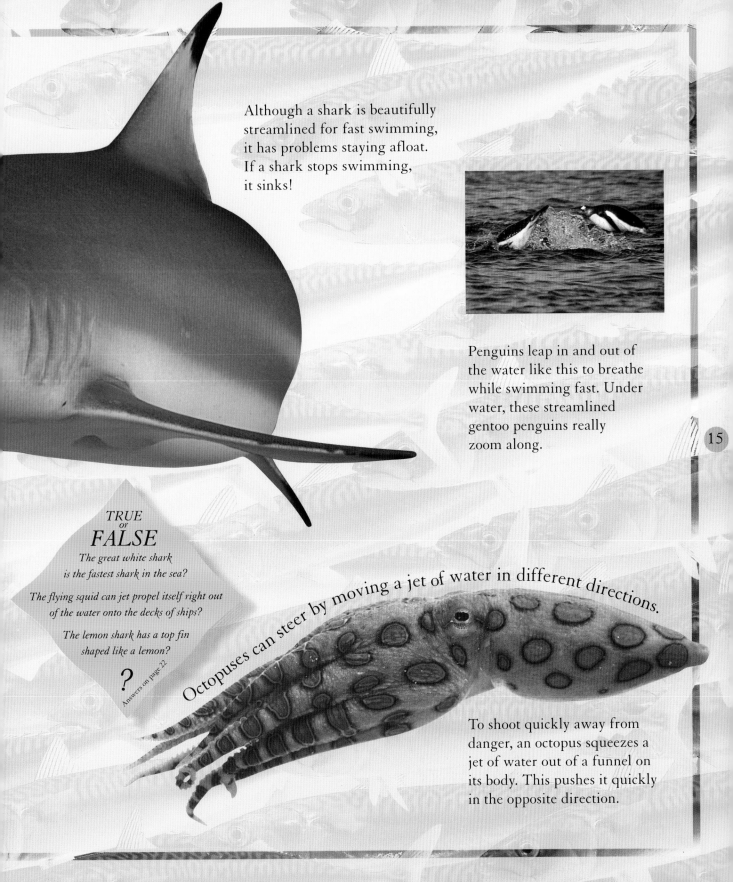

Although a shark is beautifully streamlined for fast swimming, it has problems staying afloat. If a shark stops swimming, it sinks!

Penguins leap in and out of the water like this to breathe while swimming fast. Under water, these streamlined gentoo penguins really zoom along.

TRUE
or
FALSE

The great white shark is the fastest shark in the sea?

The flying squid can jet propel itself right out of the water onto the decks of ships?

The lemon shark has a top fin shaped like a lemon?

? Answers on page 22

Octopuses can steer by moving a jet of water in different directions.

To shoot quickly away from danger, an octopus squeezes a jet of water out of a funnel on its body. This pushes it quickly in the opposite direction.

Green travelers

Although plants cannot walk, swim or fly, they use the wind, water or animal "messengers" to move their seeds away from the parent plants. Some seeds even zoom away on little rockets or catapults.

The seeds of pine trees ripen inside the woody cones. In warm, dry weather the cone opens and the seeds fall out. The wind blows some of them away.

Birds eat the red "berries" of yew trees and fly away with them. The seeds in the berries come out in the birds' droppings.

TRUE
or
FALSE

The seed pods of a squirting cucumber can shoot out as far as 6 yards?

After a year floating in the sea, sea bean seeds can still sprout into new plants on land?

Maple seeds fly through the air like jet planes?

?

Answers on page 22

The seed containers of the huru tree explode and hurl the seeds for distances up to 15 feet. Because of the loud bang this makes, the huru tree is also called the monkey's dinner bell.

Himalayan balsam catapults its seeds away. When the ripe seed case is moved by the wind, or touched by an animal, it suddenly curls up and flicks out its seeds.

The African grapple plant has sharp, strong hooks on its seeds. These hooks allow the seeds to cling to an animal's fur or feet, and hitch a free ride.

The yellow flag relies on water to carry its seeds away. The shiny brown seeds have air-filled coats which help them to float on the water.

Have you ever tried blowing on a dandelion clock? The seeds have parachutes of fluffy white hairs that help them to float away.

Water power

The formidable power of water can dramatically change the shape of the land. Winding rivers slowly grind away the rocks around them, and torrential waterfalls crash to the ground, pounding away the land.

The awesome landscape of the Grand Canyon (left), in North America, took about 6 million years to form. The canyon was carved out by the Colorado River, together with ice, wind and the rain.

As water tumbles over a steep cliff of rock, it comes crashing down at high speed to make a foaming white curtain that sparkles in the sun. The water falls so fast that it breaks up into clouds of spray.

The Grand Canyon is so deep that it takes a whole day to walk from the top to the bottom. The rocks at the top are about 250 million years old. The rocks at the bottom are an incredible 1,250 million years old.

Did You Know?

The world's biggest waterfall is under the sea, between Iceland and Greenland. Water drops more than 2 miles!

Big waves in Hawaii can crash onto the shore at 25 miles per hour.

Whizzing winds

With whirling winds that spin round at 250-500 miles per hour, tornadoes or twisters are the fastest winds on the planet. Other speedy winds are hurricanes and cyclones. All these whizzing winds happen when big parcels of warm and cold air meet, or there is lots of heat and moisture in the air.

Strong stormy winds make it difficult to walk, or even to stand up!

A dust devil is a mini-whirlwind in the desert. A spinning funnel of hot air rises up, taking dust and sand with it.

TRUE
or
FALSE

*In Tucson, Arizona, there
are about 80 dust devils a day?*

*Fish, frogs and dogs have all fallen
out of tornadoes?*

*High-speed trains can
create tornadoes?*

?

Answers on page 22

Tornadoes are like giant
vacuum cleaners, sucking
up everything in their path.
They hang down from
thunderclouds, and tear
along with a screaming,
hissing noise.

A tornado is dark at the bottom
because of all the debris it picks
up on its way.

Index

True or False answers

Runners and jumpers
★ True, it can run at 45 miles per hour, while a human
   sprinter runs at about 22 miles per hour.
★ False, a jumping spider can jump about 40 times
   the length of its own body though.
★ False, a race horse runs at up to 43 miles per hour,
   a cheetah at up to 54 miles per hour.

Speedy swimmers
★ False, the fastest is the shortfin mako.
★ True.
★ False, but the belly is yellow!

Green travelers
★ True.
★ True.
★ False, they spin like helicopter blades.

Whizzing winds
★ True.
★ True.
★ False, but fast-flying aircraft can create a kind
   of mini-tornado.